# Linking In to Pay it Forward:

## Changing the Value Proposition in Social Media

By

Chuck Hester

## About Chuck Hester

Chuck Hester is a national and international speaker on the subject of using social media for branding, media relations and helping others. A communications professional with more than 30 years experience, he is the Communications Director for iContact, an email marketing software company in Durham, North Carolina.

Chuck and his wife Stephanie are hosts of LinkedIn Live Raleigh, a networking event that regularly attracts more than 350 professionals and helps others pay it forward in person.

Chuck's website, The Pay it Forward Chronicles, can be found at www.chuckhester.com

**Linking In To Pay It Forward**

ISBN: 978-0-9728638-0-3

The author may be contacted at: chuck@chuckhester.com

Cover Design by: Elissa James
http://elissajames.synthasite.com

First Printing: May 2009
Printed in the United States of America

10 9 8 7 6 5 4 3 2 1

## Dedication:

There are several people I must thank for helping me make this book a reality.

To Paul Gillin, an old friend resurfaced, who nudged me along and convinced me that people wanted to hear what I had to say. Thanks old friend, I still want to grow up to be you!

Albert Maruggi, whose call Christmas Week got me off my duff and back on the computer to write. You're my favorite Italian in the Twin Cities!

To Christopher Morrissette – your help made this book a reality. Your friendship was not requested but is most welcome.

To Jack Tackett – I came to you for advice and came away with a great friend. Thanks for helping me with this project.

Shel Holtz, Kristie Wells and Chris Heuer, Chris Brogan, Brian Solis and other social media pros that believed in what I had to say and convinced me to make this project a reality. Thank you folks for letting me be part of the group.

To James Wong and Taylor Barr, comrades in social media arms at iContact. Thanks to you, work is a fun place to be.

To Ryan Allis and Aaron Houghton – it's been an amazing ride, guys. I'm proud to be part of the iContact team and to work side by side with two inspiring entrepreneurs.

To all of those who have attended LinkedIn Live, to our sponsors – especially Sheldon and Matt from the Select Group and Jimmy Goodman and Rick Smith of WRAL/Capital Broadcasting.  Thanks for letting us Pay it Forward.

To Marlon Headen, Wes Elder, Eric Dykes, Greg Bennett, Greg Hyer, Matt Allen and all of my other amazing in-person connections who let me ramble on and convinced me to continue to move forward.  You're the best guys, and the ones I want to end the evening with at our LinkedIn Live functions.

To my daughters, Lizz, Sarah and Britini – I know you're still not sure what Dad does for a living.  Maybe this book will help a little! Thanks for being rays of sunshine in my life.

To my Mom and Dad, Charles and Virginia Hester.  Your presence in my life will always be special to me and our family.

Finally, to the best partner a guy could ever have – in business, in life and in love – Stephanie Hester.  I couldn't ask for a better companion on this journey.  I can't wait for what's yet to come.  I love you more than I can say and know that I was blessed the day we met.

Thank You.


Chuck Hester

May, 2009

# Table of Contents

This is NOT Your Daddy's Business Book .............. 1

Building your brand – a practical guide .............. 11

Treat Them Like They're Right in Front of You -
Online social media etiquette ........................... 17

Want to Meet for Coffee?  Putting the Social Back
Into Social Media ............................................. 23

Stories from LinkedIn Live ................................. 29

Paying it Forward – How Can I be of Service to
YOU? ............................................................... 39

In Conclusion .................................................... 49

## This is NOT Your Daddy's Business Book

Since I was a kid I have always been a networker. I remember grabbing my mom's Women's Club directory and cold calling all her fellow members to buy grapefruit to raise money for a church choir trip – and bringing in over $900 in the process – a king's ransom in 1975.

I have been in high tech public relations since 1984, working for everyone from Western Digital to TEAC to the Department of Defense Technology Transfer Program to my best and current job as Communications Direct for iContact Corporation.

That's 28 years of booms and busts, fads and favorites, the "new" Mac, Yahoo, and that small upstart called Google. Throughout those 28 years, one thing has been constant for me – I always had an affinity for connecting with other people.

Before online networking, I was known for my ability to find someone, get an answer to a question, all within three phone calls. This was before Google, or even Yahoo search. Lexus/Nexus was just coming into being in the late 1980s.

I was always told I was good with people, could talk to anyone and later that I "never met a microphone I didn't like." So, when the Internet took hold for good, and being online was the way to go, I felt that social networking was made just for me.

At first it was a way to connect online, with reservations. There were things that this corporate/agency raised professional didn't like. Tell them your intimate details? Meet people online anywhere anytime in anyplace? But they're not standing in front of you, how can that work well?

But slowly I became accustomed to this new business tool. There was LinkedIn, Facebook, Plaxo, even Yahoo Groups. All had their plusses, and many had their minuses.

It wasn't until I joined iContact in July of 2006 that I realized the power of social media – and online networking - and how important it would become in my life.

As iContact's first PR Director, I was charged with building a Social Media plan, reaching out to bloggers and making our company known in the online community. It was a process where I learned as I went, but I drew on my strength of being able to connect to people. It made all the difference in the world.

Through social networking, I have developed friendships that will last a lifetime, found partners and business for iContact and garnered media coverage in major media outlets – both on and off-line. This includes the New York Times, Wall Street Journal and Fast Company.com.

I have refinanced my house using a broker I found, and connected friends with key executives of companies that they wanted to reach. I have received offers to speak at conferences, and my wife even found the right shoes to wear when conducting Team Building seminars!

Maybe just as important, I have built a business and personal brand that is recognized throughout the U.S. and continues to reach others outside of the United States.

Oh, and one other detail – I met my CEO, Ryan Allis, and got my job as a direct result of connecting with him through social media.  Plus, I learned a thing or two from him on how to pay it forward.

All from one website – LinkedIn.

Over the past 2 ½ years I have slowly grown my LinkedIn network to where it stands today – more than 8500 direct connections in every state in the United States, Europe,

Asia, Australia and Africa, Canada and South America.

To put that in perspective, I have the ability to directly reach more than 8500 people in companies ranging from IBM to Microsoft to Starbucks. With LinkedIn I can email them directly or even message them through the application.

With this tremendous network I can now reach out to practically anywhere in the world, to almost any industry. When I travel I always enjoy the company of my LinkedIn connections. I have been able to assist in getting jobs for more than 40 people to date through LinkedIn Live Raleigh – an in-person LinkedIn networking event I started in July, 2007.

I truly believe LinkedIn is the best way to network online – and to Pay it Forward.

Again, more about that and other topics surrounding my passion later in this book.

First, as the chapter title implies, this is NOT your Daddy's business book.  I'm not going to give you a series of exercises to make you a better networker.  Nor am I going to run you through a step-by-step process on how to use LinkedIn as a web application.

There are plenty of good websites and books that can do that as well, if not better than I.  Jason Alba's *I'm on LinkedIn Now What?* is the best example.

No, this is more of a "let's sit down and talk" story.  A way to help you realize the power of Linking in and Paying it Forward by hearing from me and the stories of others about how we made it happen.

I will also share with you how once I started asking "how can I be of service to you?" instead of wanting to know "what can you do for me?" when I connected with people on LinkedIn, the value proposition of social media changed for me – for the better.

My hope is that you will come away from this inspired, hungry for more information and ready to enrich your life, and the lives of others, through social networking.

Another thing this book is not – long and drawn out.  My good friend, Rich Sloan, who was one of the many that pushed me to write this book, said I should use the Seth Godin model of less is more.  Nuggets instead of full course meals. I couldn't agree more.

This book is a chance for me to share the good fortune that I have enjoyed as a result of using LinkedIn, and hopefully touch a few people along the way.

One more thing, many people I connect with ask me if my Pay it Forward philosophy is inspired by the book and then the movie of the same name. In a way, yes, but my inspiration comes more from the blessings my wife Stephanie and I have received from those that helped us. We believe it's important for us to continually pay it forward to other so that we can make this world – business and personal – a better place to live.

With that being said, let's get started.

# - 2 -

## Building your brand – a practical guide

*Step-by-step details on how to build your brand using social media and LinkedIn*

How important is branding building to your success? Is building your brand a costly proposition? What about tying your company/service into your personal brand – is that suggested, or for that matter wise? I will answer these, and many other questions in this chapter.

While I didn't start out using LinkedIn and other social media channels to build my own brand (I was looking for a job first and foremost) I did find that as I built up my online presence my brand was being bolstered at the same time.

LinkedIn is, just like other social media sites, primarily a community of people. There are real, living and breathing individuals behind the profiles. They have conversations, interact, and rely on the trust that is built through these interactions.

Can you build a personal brand overnight? Not hardly. It takes time, just like any relationship – business or otherwise – to establish a presence in a community.

My brand has been built over the last three years. I have contributed to forums on LinkedIn, asked and answered questions on the Answers section of the site. Connected with hundreds of people, meeting them online and in person. As daunting as building a brand on LinkedIn may sound, there are a few easy steps to make it happen. The old saying – the best way to eat an elephant is one bite at a time –

comes to mind. Take it slow and follow a few simple steps, and you'll be on your way!

**Be Transparent**  Does this mean you talk about your love life or how you yelled at your kid last night because they broke curfew? Hardly! But it does mean simply be yourself. Don't put on a "persona." I had a conversation with someone recently about how they were developing what they would portray themselves to be online. Wow! Not someone I want to hang out with! If you aren't real online, how can I trust you to do business with me in an ethical manner?

**Be Part of the Community**  Join a group that interests you. Answer questions, and ask them in the Answers section. Invite others to connect with you after reading their profiles and finding commonality. In short, join the conversation!

**Practice the Small Good** This theory – a parallel to Pay it Forward – is one of my favorites. If someone comes to you and needs help – and it takes less than 10 minutes to help them, by all means do it! The result is a huge blessing for the person who was stumped and couldn't find the help he needed. Easy to do, very valuable to receive.

**Go into any connection on LinkedIn not expecting to get anything in return**. IF you go into a new connection and immediately expect them to be helpful, then that can ruin the trust you are working to establish. If, on the other hand, you go into a new connection with the attitude of how you can help them it will be a richer, deeper relationship.

**Always treat your connections like they're standing right in front of you**  While I'll get more specific in the next chapter about this, I wanted to mention it here because I believe it's that important. If you go to a business function – say a Chamber business after hours – do you approach new contacts with canned speeches and personas? Do you walk up to them and say, "Hi, I'm Chuck. I work for Acme Life Insurance, want to buy some?" No, you take the time to get to know them, learn about their businesses, perhaps even their families. What's more you follow up with them after the meeting if you want to build on the connection and continue to the conversation.

It's the same with social media. NEVER connect with someone, then turn around and ask for them to recommend you. Take the time to get to know them, find out how you can be of SERVICE to them. It will pay off in the end.

I am a firm believer that the person you connect with is probably not the one that will mean new business for you. It's that person's other connections – or even the connections of their connections.

Bottom line on personal and professional branding: be yourself, be a resource, build trust and treat your online connections like their real – they are!

# - 3 -

## Treat Them Like They're Right in Front of You - Online social media etiquette

Tips for interacting online in social media

Here's the scenario: A person contacts you and would like to get to know you better, on a business level. You agree and start a conversation. As the relationship develops you find that you have more things in common than you originally thought. You want to deepen the relationship. You look for ways to help this other person and become good friends. Oh, and by the way, you've never actually physically met.

Welcome to the world of online networking. For this old-fashioned guy, it took a while to get used to meeting and talking to folks for months, sometimes years that I never actually met. Until I decide to apply a very important principal to my online relationships:

**_Treat your connections like they're standing right in front of you._**

By using your inherent sense of respect for others, you can develop some amazing relationships online.

Here's a few tips that can help your connections like they're standing right in front of you:

**Be open to new relationships** I often get invitations on LinkedIn from people I have nothing in common with – an IT administrator, a blogging mom in New Hampshire – and for the most part I always accept those invitations. Why? Because I never know what may come out of that relationship in the long run.

**Be polite but be honest** Respond back to invitations honestly. IF you don't want to pursue the relationship, then say so.

**Be yourself and be who you are, not who you want others to think you are** Don't put on an online "identity" to impress or try and influence.

**Remember the other person is real – not just a computer connection**  Respond in a reasonable time, don't ignore them and be sure to follow through on anything you commit to do.

**Listen, don't just talk**  Listening is an art not easily mastered, especially in the white noise world of online networking!

**Finally, look for ways to develop an online relationship into a physical one**  Like the person you're connected to – either as a friend or business associate? Then take the time to meet them if you can. Make the face to face connection.

So, my question to you is simple: Who are you connected to online that you don't know well but who may make a difference in your life? More importantly, who are you connected to online that you can make a difference in THEIR lives?

# - 4 -

## Want to Meet for Coffee?  Putting the Social Back Into Social Media

Ways to leverage your connections to develop business and personal relationships off-line

So you're actively involved in social media, meeting new contacts, being part of the community, contributing to the dialogue. For the most part, this is not face to face conversation.  It's either through the LinkedIn site, or if you take it one step further, through email and phone calls with connections you really have an affinity for and want to get to know better.

I would challenge you - today - to put the social back in social media.

While I am fascinated by the number of connections I have developed over the last several years through LinkedIn, the ones that are the deepest, most meaningful seem to be the ones I've met in person.

I mentioned Albert Maruggi in the dedication. Add to that list Shel Holtz, Mark Ragan, Doc Kane, Steven Bauer from Edelman - all connections I developed through LinkedIn and all folks who I have met in person and developed a stronger relationship as a result.

I am still perplexed by the online mentality that connecting in person - while "nice" is not necessary. I disagree.

The next chapter will detail LinkedIn Live Raleigh. Through this event, I have brought together more than 2000 people in the last two years. It started as a way to meet my LinkedIn connections locally in the Raleigh/Durham area.  A restaurant, no admission charge and three hours of solid networking.

Over the past year it has become a phenomenon.  Our latest event in March, 2009 brought 300 people together to network, pay it forward and help each other out.  More on LI Live in the next chapter...

So how do you go about putting the social back in social media? I suggest you apply the rules of good old fashion business networking and apply it to your online connections.

1. If you connect with someone in your local area through LinkedIn and there's an affinity, suggest a meeting in person. Be open to what might come out of that meeting. Be prepared, as well, that nothing may happen.

2. When you travel - conferences, seminars, even for pleasure - check your LinkedIn connections list to see if there are connections in the city you are going to that you'd like to meet. I have done this for over two years now, meeting either one-on-one or in groups with my connections. No agenda (see a pattern) just meeting to find out more about each other.

3. Be willing to take it one step at a time.  Start with a phone call or a series of emails.  You can discover, sometimes that there isn't any chemistry and it doesn't make sense for you to meet.  That's okay, too, by the way.  You can say no to a connection.

4. Accept requests for your advice or guidance.  This is one of my favorite ways to pay it forward.  If someone asks to meet just to hear about my experiences, I will - at the minimum - meet with them at least once to see if I can help.

Social media is truly "social" first and media second.  We often emphasize the technology, the widget, new application or wiz bang way to communicate.

If we are not social and friend, if we don't participate in the social networks we use through dialog and interaction, then we might as well stay behind our computer screens and send out canned messages when contacted.

But hey, what's the joy in that? My favorite part of social media is finally meeting a good connection in person. Seeing them for the first time and greeting them like a long lost friend!

Next, LinkedIn Live - the stories will amaze you. My wife Stephanie and I love these events as our way of paying it forward!

# - 5 -

## Stories from LinkedIn Live

Particular stories from LinkedIn Live – my networking event that attracts 300 people

LinkedIn Live Raleigh started in July of 2007 as a way to meet my LinkedIn connections that lived in the Raleigh area all at once. I was having coffee with Wes Elder, a good friend now – and getting to know what previously had been an online only connection. We both lamented that we were doing these "get to know you" coffees about 3 times a week and felt there had to be a better way. Thus LinkedIn Live was born.

Several things have contributed to the
success of LinkedIn Live Raleigh – not the
least of which was coverage by the Raleigh
News & Observer by Sue Stock (also now a
good friend) of the first meeting. The story
landed on the front page of the business
section and we have never looked back.

I am a true believer in two things: Word of
Mouth marketing and the pay it forward
philosophy (more on that in the next
chapter). LinkedIn Live has enjoyed some
amazing word of mouth, resulting in an
increase in attendance from 50 to well over
300 in the past 18 months. No one thought
it would grow like it has, especially not me.

But, at the heart of LinkedIn Live is our
ability to pay it forward for so many in the
local Raleigh area. It's been a joy to put on

the semi-monthly events and very gratifying to see how many lives it has touched.

While there may be a second book just on LinkedIn Live stories – I wanted to share a few here as an illustration of the power of LinkedIn – and paying it forward.

At each LinkedIn Live we give away a number of door prizes – dinners, tickets to concerts.  It is, as I put it at a recent event, like playing Santa Claus. We have very generous door prize donors, and greatly appreciate them coming forward to help.

One giveaway was a certificate for $75 for a local restaurant. While you never know how this can impact someone, we soon found out. The winner of this prize was a gentleman who, after winning the prize, stopped my wife to explain why winning meant so much to him.

He told Stephanie: "I was just laid off last week, and was not in a great place. On top of that, my birthday AND my anniversary are less than 10 days away. Losing my job was preventing me from celebrating with my wife and family. This gift allows me to do so. It means SO much to me."

Both Stephanie – when she heard this – and I – when she told me later about it – took this as validation of why we do what we do. If we can give back, through door prizes, bringing people into a room to network, or just helping them understand how to use LinkedIn better to network – we are blessed by the results.

Last summer, at a LinkedIn Live event, we gave away a special door prize that was in honor of Dress for Success – a national charity that helps women get work clothes for interviews and for their first week on the job. The winner of that prize came up to me afterwards and told me it must have been meant to be. "I've been trying to find the organizers of the local Dress for Success chapter," he explained. "Our firm wants to donate to them on a regular basis but didn't know who to contact. Now we do!"

With the recent downturn in the economy, networking – whether it be online or in-person – has become more important than ever. The ability to get out and meet contacts that can make the difference for you is key.

Our philosophy for continuing with LinkedIn Live has been simple – bring people together so they can help each other.

At last count, more than 40 people have found their current jobs as a result of meeting people at LinkedIn Live events. Countless numbers of business relationships have been formed – many resulting in business deals worth thousands of dollars.

To date, there are more than 20 LinkedIn Live events around the country, including Warsaw, Poland. Some of the organizers have contacted me before they started their events to get a few tips, but for the most part it has been a grass roots movement.

Now, here's where I get to stand on my soap box. Stephanie and I were effectively unemployed for close to three years during the dotcom bubble burst and 9/11. Every cent was precious to us, but we knew we had to network to find work.

Because of this, we are extremely sensitive to what finding a job can cost an individual. We have never charged a dime to attend a LinkedIn Live – and we never will. There are those who charge for "how to network" seminars and meetings on how to use LinkedIn. To me, that's missing the true meaning of networking.

If you aren't willing to pay it forward, put yourself out there and help someone – then you're only in it for the money, and I believe that's the wrong way of doing things.

### *Stepping down off the soapbox*

One other side benefit of LinkedIn Live? Friendships that are deeper and more meaningful than if they were just online. As I mentioned in the last chapter, I truly believe it's important to emphasize the "social" in social media.

My friends and I connect online on a regular basis. But, a core group of us look forward to every other month's LinkedIn Live to meet in person, have a drink and talk to each other face to face.

No computer program, newest app or video blogging application can ever replace a friend's smile and handshake. That's a treasure that can't be programmed or coded.

The next chapter will discuss the pay it forward philosophy in detail, along with some personal examples that I have experienced – as well as others' stories.

# - 6 -

## Paying it Forward – How Can I be of Service to YOU?

For many, living a pay it forward lifestyle doesn't take a great deal of effort.  It's something you do every day.  In fact, you may be paying it forward without consciously knowing you are, and without knowing that you're making a difference.

Have you ever been at the grocery store and the person in front of you was short on the bill?  Did you reach into your wallet and make up the difference?  That's the first part of paying it forward.

How about seeing a cop at a coffee shop and paying for her coffee?  That's the start of paying it forward.

The fundamental difference, as I see it, is that in order to truly pay it forward you must always want to help another person without:

1. Ever expecting anything in return and

2. Letting the person who did you the "favor" know that you expect them to pay it forward to someone else.

For me, that is how I help other people by paying it forward.  It's relatively easy to do someone a favor – the way that we help more than one person is by encouraging others to pass that favor on – or pay it forward!

Today's amazingly connected online world is what I believe to be the best pay it forward playground in history.  We have never been able to reach as many people through as many modes of communication than we can today.  LinkedIn is just one of many great online communities that put you in touch with so many people around the world.

Through LinkedIn, as I have touched on in earlier chapters in this book, I have developed friendships, business relationships and lifelong partnerships that would have not been available to me offline.  As I'm writing this chapter I'm on my way to Sydney, Australia.   I'm speaking at an Innovations Conference.  A speaking engagement I secured through connecting with the Conference chair on LinkedIn.

Granted, to get where I am now has taken a lot of hard work, a lot of perseverance and in no small measure – a lot of faith.  But it's also been a result of my use of LinkedIn to reach out to new connections and hopefully make a small difference along the way.

My point is simple: if you are using social media, you should be using it to pay it forward.  You have no good excuse, in my opinion.

When you connect with someone – on LinkedIn, Facebook, Twitter – wherever you may meet them – ALWAYS go into the relationship with the thought that you are about to pay it forward.

Think about it. If you know that by connecting with a person you have the potential to help them in some way aren't you excited about what might happen? Doesn't it make you anticipate what you can do?

For me, and my many connections (at the time I'm writing this chapter around 10,000 on LinkedIn, Facebook and Twitter combined) it is a new adventure every time we connect.

Several men and women are role models for me in the pay it forward life that I have chosen to lead. Some are well known, some not so well known, and some are totally satisfied just being there when someone needs help.

In the last four years I have had the privilege to not only know, but call friends, great people such as Paul Gillin, Chris Brogan, Kristie Wells and Chris Heuer, Jen McClure, Steve Bauer, Shel Holtz, Mark Ragan, Seth Godin, Wes Elder, Eric Dykes, Christopher Morrisette, Marlon Headen, Greg Bennett, Greg Hyer, Matt Zaske, Sheldon Wolitski, and so many others it would take another chapter just to list them.

All of them have one thing in common – they rarely said no. To a request for an introduction, a chance to sit and talk over coffee. But, most importantly, they never – to the person – ever said no when I asked them to pay it forward and help someone else.

The best part of paying it forward?  Once you get in the habit it is easy to do and a very hard habit to break!

So, if you have come this far and read this chapter, then it's time for me to issue the challenge.  (Which by the way thrills me to no end that I have the "platform" to do so).

Okay, here it is – the Linking In to Pay it Forward Challenge:

After you finish this book, take a minute to reach out to five of your connections.  Talk to them through LinkedIn, Twitter, Facebook, email or *GASP* the phone.  Find out if they have a particular need that you can help them with TODAY.

Some will say no, but thanks.  But I imagine several will say yes, and lay it out for you right then and there.

If you can't personally help, find someone you know that can, and connect them to the person in need.

Now, here's the kicker: once you done this, challenge them to find five of their connections and do the same thing.

In return, here's my pledge to you.  My website – www.chuckhester.com is subtitled The Pay it Forward Chronicles.  If you will contact me and let me know the results from your willingness to take the Linking In To Pay it Forward Challenge – I will publish as many of your stories as possible on my website.

My hope is that my next book will be devoted exclusively to these stories. Stories of paying it forward through LinkedIn and social media.

Oh, and one more thing. If you want to take the Linking In to Pay it Forward Challenge and are stuck on who to ask, contact me and I'll help you get started!

A side note – in the last few years I have developed a reputation for answering the emails  and the connection requests I received without fail.  My only caveat has always been if you're selling me something, you're a spammer or you can't find the time to personalize your requests, then I will either ask you to introduce yourself in a more personal way, or I'll pass and not connect.

I mention this only to assure you that if you do contact me with a story, I will read it and most likely let my readers know about it.   I also will help you out should you need it.

My heartfelt hope is that my story has somehow touched you in a way that will inspire you to help someone else.

# - 7 -

## In Conclusion

I ended the last chapter with heartfelt hope. I will start this – the last chapter – with another heartfelt hope. I promised you that this would not be your typical business book. My hope is that you have enjoyed it as a story, while at the same time finding a few things you can apply to your business life.

The old business presentation adage – tell them what you're going to tell them; tell them; then tell them what you told them – should probably apply to this chapter.

Of all the phrases that can be cliché but so true here is this – what are the "takeaways."

Here are few that I hope you picked up on:

1. Treat your connections like they're standing right in front of you

2. Be part of the community

3. Connect to the connectors

4. Strive to put the Social in Social Media

5. Always ask how you can be of service to a new connection

6. Take the meeting – you never know what may come out of it

7. Don't be afraid to ask – you'll be surprised how many people will say "yes!"

8. Our world is more connected than any time in history thanks to social media We should take advantage of this – and take the privilege seriously.

9. Be consistent online – never "put on a persona"

10. Pay it forward is a lifestyle – and a great habit that is hard to break

Finally, I hope to connect with you in some form or another in the future. My LinkedIn connections are yours. Connect with me through LinkedIn, Twitter and Facebook. Email me directly. As I mentioned I'll answer everyone that's sincere.

My wife, Stephanie, and I have been blessed. Blessed with friends and relationships richer than we could have imagined. The best part is that we believe that this is only the beginning. That what we can accomplish by paying it forward through LinkedIn and social media we can't even begin to comprehend.

So, my wish for you is more of the same...great connections, great friendships and a chance to pay it forward all over the world.

If this is our first introduction, then I hope it's the start of a great connection for both of us.

I look forward to meeting you – online and in-person – and hearing your stories of linking in to pay it forward.

Until then, remember:


Stay well, stay connected, and continue to Pay it Forward!

## Pay it Forward Stories Wanted!

My next book is called the Pay it Forward Chronicles: Stories of Linking In to Pay it Forward. I welcome you to be part of this book!

If you are paying it forward using social networking, then I want to hear from you.

Send an email to chuck@chuckhester.com and tell me about your experiences.

Your stories will be posted on my website – www.chuckhester.com and compiled in a collection to be published later this year.